life, love and loss
Pathways to Peace and Possibilities

RICHARD W. HALLSTEIN

Copyright © 2014 Richard W. Hallstein

All rights reserved. This book or any portion thereof may not be reproduced or used in any manner whatsoever without express permission of the publisher except for the use of brief quotations in a book review.

First Printing, 2014

ISBN: 978-0692311646

Available for re-order via Amazon.com

Printed in the United States of America

DEDICATION

For 35 years, my wife, Karen Moran, was the love of my life and my cherished development partner. Day by day and year by year, we supported each other's growth and development; challenged each other to be the best that we could be; sought out learning opportunities in locations far and wide; laughed, danced and sang; and provided one another love and support during all of life's challenges. We had the special privilege and joy of working together and with family members, friends and clients to discover and co-create new possibilities for satisfying, contributing relationships, lives and work.

Karen was diagnosed with leukemia in May of 2012 and passed away in November 2013. Our partnership of love and learning continued to the very end. And her guidance and voice has been clear and present for me as I attempt to share some of what she helped me learn about life, love and loss.

Karen's beloved sister, Patty Moran, who was intimately and lovingly involved with us during Karen's diagnosis, treatment and passing continues as a competent and caring support to me. She helps keep Karen's presence and voice alive in me; provides on-going companionship, love and encouragement; and she is the best reader and editor that anyone could hope to have available.

I dedicate this book to these loving sisters and hope that what they have made it possible for me to express in this book illuminates a pathway to peace and possibilities for others navigating life's joys and challenges.

KAREN MORAN LEADERSHIP FUND

All author proceeds from the sale of this book will go to the fund established to honor the memory of the author's deceased wife, Karen Moran.

Karen led with uncommon courage and integrity, fueled by a fierce passion for many diverse perspectives, particularly under-represented voices.

This fund will carry forward Karen's dream of strengthening the leadership capacity of women and girls of all races and classes, allowing them to reach their full potential.

This is a dedicated fund associated with the Maine Women's Fund. Additional contributions can be addressed to:

Karen Moran, 1951 - 2013

Karen Moran Leadership Fund
Maine Women's Fund
74 Lunt Road
Suite 100
Falmouth, ME 04105

MIRROR AND FACE

We are the mirror as well as the face in it.

We are tasting the taste this minute
of eternity. We are pain
and what cures pain, both.

We are the sweet cold water and the jar that pours.

~ Rumi

TABLE OF CONTENTS

Introduction	13
Chapter 1: On Being Spiritual	15
Chapter 2: Impermanence	19
Chapter 3: Surrender	23
Chapter 4: Prayer	27
Chapter 5: Love	31
Chapter 6: Being Present	35
Chapter 7: Belief	39
Chapter 8: Karma	43
Chapter 9: Desire	47
Chapter 10: Stillness	51
Chapter 11: Embodiment	55
Chapter 12: Relationship Investing	59
Chapter 13: Expressing Feelings	63
Chapter 14: Change	67
Chapter 15: Rituals	71
Chapter 16: No-Self	75
Chapter 17: Compassion	79
Conclusion: It's Never Too Late	83

INTRODUCTION

None of us gets out of this life alive! Those of us who have arrived at or survived middle age are faced with that harsh reality and several others that we must either deal with or deny. Almost none of us has avoided the pain of lost friends, family and loves. Most have to reconcile significant changes in the scope, intensity or impact of our roles in the world or workplace. We may watch our centrality to the lives of our kids shift, as they carry on with their careers, lives and families of their own. At some time, we may find ourselves facing changes in our physical or mental capabilities.

Though many folks are hit with painful changes and losses early in life, the accumulation of these events often accelerates as we get older. These changes can catch us by surprise, knock the wind out of our sails and derail us physically and emotionally. Yet, some have followed paths that seem to make them better able to weather these life storms. They seem to be able to fully experience their grief and loss while sustaining their underlying love of life and optimism about the future.

Throughout our lives, we all make some level of conscious and unconscious investment in practices that will enliven us during the good times and support us in times of loss and grief. Some turn to religion or other spiritual paths. Others invest in personal growth and therapy. Still others expect to rely on deep and nourishing relationships. Sustenance and support can also be found in meaningful work and supporting social, political and environmental causes. Art and music may be our refuge.

Over the past three years, I lost my wife, 18 months after she was diagnosed with leukemia. I ended the traveling part of a 30-year consulting career that took me to many exciting places in the US and around the world. After 47 years of running, where I logged enough miles to have circled the globe twice, I had to yield to some physical signals that said, "It's time to hang up the running shoes." And, upon turning 74, I have had to come to grips with becoming a member of the "young old." All of these losses have reverberated throughout my body, mind and spirit.

In past decades and during this more challenging recent journey, I have been blessed to have family, friends, guides and teachers who helped me find and commit to practices that have allowed me to develop a more peaceful relationship to the joys, loss and suffering that life brings to our doorsteps. These practices have reduced my suffering and expanded my capacity for compassion and loving kindness to myself and others.

I feel called to write this book. I feel called to examine what it is we are counting on to meet the loss and suffering that we are or will be experiencing. I want to extend an invitation to deepen existing practices; to embrace paths that may be underutilized; to recognize life activities that we may not view as practices and to elevate them to a level of consciousness that helps bring peace and loving connection to all that is around us.

Once begun, the journey never ends. We are asked to bring more attention to each moment that can evoke awe and gratitude for this great mystery and gift of life. We are called upon to deepen our understanding of our intentions, behaviors and impact on others. And there is the never-ending mental roller coaster of trying to stay in the moment, so that we do not miss the peace, love and contact that eludes us, when we are rewinding to the past or fast forwarding to the future.

This is not a book of promises. This is a book that hopes to shed some light on possibilities. I'm referring to the possibilities that emerge when we make a move toward embracing the sacred potential in all of life's daily activities, even when we are overcome by loss and grief. While mundane, there is beauty in a shower or a meal; working in the yard; holding hands and watching TV; knitting; working with your daughter on her homework; or accepting the loving gift of a meal delivered by a friend.

The book is organized into a series of mini-chapters for reflection and contemplation. They can be read sequentially or randomly. Each chapter represents a special learning from my personal journey. There are some themes that run throughout and, by necessity, there is some overlap.

There are some thoughts for your contemplation, meditation or action following each mini-chapter.

I'm grateful to be on the path and to share it with you. I have no sense of personal mastery of the path. However, I feel as though I have stepped through the door, see the road ahead and am joyous to have your partnership on the trail.

CHAPTER ONE

ON BEING SPIRITUAL

In the past quarter-century, it has become quite familiar to hear someone say, "I'm not religious, but I am spiritual." What does that mean?

In my own case, the road from religious to claiming "spiritual" has been quite rocky. Like many others, I watched with dismay as the religions that I grew up with vilified my gay and lesbian friends and family members; disenfranchised women; overlooked the abuses of children by church leaders; and used scripture to explain all manner of actions that harmed, damned, shamed or excluded people that I loved.

In addition, far-reaching, scientific discoveries seemed to be making the case that whatever we didn't understand would become known in due time. All great mysteries were just waiting to be revealed and there was no God in Heaven to turn to for the answers. In fact, religious belief was viewed as little more than an "opiate for the masses."

There is much to be said for emancipating from any distorted manifestation of religious dogma that denies science and narrows the circle of people that receive our compassion and love. Yet, in my case, much was lost as well.

For years, I described myself as an atheist. In the 60's, I was proud to be known as a member of Madalyn Murray O'Hair's American Atheists. I defined myself primarily in terms of what I didn't believe. I had disdain for those who did believe. I could enumerate at length the atrocities perpetuated by organized religion. I was often blind to the innumerable good deeds of believers.

Personal growth, therapy and building deep and enduring relationships went a long way to soothe my psyche and provide me navigation for my life and work. Joining the Unitarian Church offered a wonderful platform for moral direction and for joining with others to advance social justice for all. Yet something was missing.

I began to speak of feeling as though I was in a spiritual wasteland. I did not find myself in enough places where I was regularly touched by the tremor of awe. Days and weeks went by when I did not engage with others in a celebration of life. The sacred reverence for the great mystery of our very existence got lost in scientific inquiry. I could make love and play music skillfully without feeling deep passion. I missed the humbling connection across the millennia to all those before us – who looked to the stars and developed ritual to relate to the mystery, terror and joy of being on this planet.

Left behind in the carnage of religious disillusionment were the art, rituals, music, community and inspiring messages of the religious houses of worship that from earlier days, in their best moments, called us to connect with that which is larger than ourselves; that humbled us in the face of the gifts that come our way; that offered opportunity to feel and experience that which cannot be measured; that connected us to eons of fellow strugglers and meaning-makers; that opened our hearts to the love that is in and around us; that called us to our best selves. That's what was missing!

It's impossible to linearly chart my path from this wasteland to "being spiritual." However, I'm comfortable saying awakening to my yearning for "what was missing" guided the journey.

So, I found myself seeking experiences that inspired awe and gratitude for this unimaginable gift of life. These experiences included large adventures like a solo, fasting vision quest in the mountains of Northern California. However, in a more modest gesture, each morning I stand on my porch, open my arms and say, "I am full of awe and gratitude." Doing so brings me daily to this reverent place.

When I am feeling like things are out of control, I sit quietly and say, "Eternal spirit, into thy loving hands I surrender my soul and destiny; may I know and lovingly respond to my calling today."

Sitting with a loved one and noticing my mind drifting to the past or future, I invite myself to be lovingly present, right here, right now. I might have to make that call three or four times, as I struggle to be present.

As the family sits down to eat, a few moments of holding hands and reflecting upon the gift of the meal and one another's presence warms the spirit.

These are a few of the practices that make each moment, day in and day out, sacred. Large adventures like vision quests may be required to awaken and put us on the path. However, it is in the micro-moments of our daily life that we have the great opportunity to live a sacred, spiritual life that is constantly experiencing awe, gratitude and loving connection, in all that we do. And in so doing, we create the possibility for double the joy and half of the grief that life brings our way.

Being on this path may require making peace with our anger and traumas from our earlier religious experiences. There is also the need to build regular habits and practice disciplines not dictated or supported by the demands of church dogma or instructions.

We might all wish for mastery of these practices. Moreover, as anyone who meditates knows, we drift and wander all over our spiritual pathway. Yet, in paying attention and returning to our path, we join hearts with all those who yearn to fall into the arms of the loving spirit in each other and the universe.

QUESTIONS: ON BEING SPIRITUAL

Thoughts for contemplation, meditation or action:

1. Do you consider yourself spiritual? Why? Why not?

2. What have you lost, if you have walked away from the religion of your youth? How might you regain some of what you lost?

3. How can you connect regularly to a sense of awe and gratitude for the gift of life?

4. What spiritual practices provide you support during times of loss? Do you need to do anything to make them more present in your life?

CHAPTER TWO

IMPERMANENCE

The sun rises and the sun falls. Flowers bloom, fade and make their way to mulch. We live and we die. Everyone is subject to the same fate. Our days are numbered as certainly as were the days of all those who have gone before us. We cannot cheat death. We can only hope to live with the fullness that the acceptance of death can bring.

There are those who find comfort in a belief in life after death. Others feel that they are part of a grand larger consciousness to which they will return. Some report having no fear of the prospect of nothingness. I deeply respect these experiences, feelings and beliefs of others. However, in my case, I feel compelled to humbly surrender and say, "Death is certain, but I have no idea what else is out there."

As a younger person, I became quite upset as the certainty of death blossomed in my awareness. The prospect of facing nothingness was scary. My uncertainty and fear manifested in a series of hypochondriacal illnesses, during which I was certain that I would die sooner, rather than later. I met this fear by launching a life-long commitment to physical fitness. This distraction from the inevitable truth served me well. As the years rolled by, I enjoyed good health and I could insulate myself from the reality of entering the fourth quarter of my life.

Other ways that fear or denial of mortality seemed to drive me and others included strong desires to leave behind monuments to our accomplishments and contributions. Many friends have said, "I don't want to die yet. I have so much to do."

Fear, denial or resistance to the impermanence of everything can lead to a sense of "I-ness" that separates us from others and the world at large. It's almost as though we are the only ones doing the dying. Mired in denial, fear or isolation, we can miss the warm embrace of sharing with others the joy and grief of this existential reality, as we make our way toward our certain end. We can miss the fact that "We are nature!" We are part of the flowing river of existence with all sentient beings and everything else that appears and then passes.

Practices to embrace impermanence can free us from the endless struggle with passing conditions and phenomena. These practices show us how to play, love and celebrate the gift of life every day, in the face of our honest acceptance that time is short. They bring attention to the thin boundary between us and everybody and everything around us and our shared destiny.

Rituals that honor the presence and passing of seasons, careers and lives provide a healing antidote to a lifetime of losses.

Some speak of detachment as a way to deal with the losses, pains and inevitable death that we all face. Though others may view it differently, the dictionary defines detachment as "avoiding emotional involvement." Paradoxically, I would recommend full, all-out, unrestrained emotional involvement with all that is impermanent. Yes, it is necessary to both hold on and then let go. I choose to experience the enormous loss when things pass, rather than to not feel every delicious moment of available lifetime contact.

During the course of our lives, we can all choose to embrace and celebrate every moment, the wonderful and the terrible. And when the time comes for lives to end, we can say "Wow, that was a good run. I would have signed up for this deal at the beginning, even knowing it would all come to an end someday."

QUESTIONS: IMPERMANENCE

Thoughts for contemplation, meditation or action:

1. Is the fact that "we all live and we all die" a large presence in your life at this time? How does that fact inform or impact your life choices?

2. What is your emotional relationship to the idea of our impermanence?

3. What do you do to celebrate each moment of life? Are there ways that you want to make this celebration of life more present for you?

4. If you could, would you have signed up for the deal (life) at the beginning, even knowing it would come to an end? Why? Why not?

CHAPTER THREE

SURRENDER

Culturally, we are hardwired to never give up, to fight the good fight and win at all costs. So, when we are called upon to surrender, it's difficult not to see that as waving a white flag in despair or admitting defeat.

A friend who has been to war is incredulous when surrender is proposed as a response to life events over which he has little control. A man in his eighties who is experiencing the loss of physical capabilities holds tenaciously onto his independence and rejects the offers of help from exasperated family members. Golfers continue to play and tempt fate as thunder and lightning flash in the background. A dear friend faces a life-threatening illness and vows to beat it. A driver who should no longer be on the road holds onto the car keys and puts himself and others at great risk.

Underlying a call to surrender is the ancient exhortation to turn things over to a power greater than ourselves. We all must define that power in any way that we understand it. However, it is an indisputable fact that we are not running the show – even though we certainly have agency and are able to influence many outcomes. The spiritual question that remains is, "When is it time to persist and when is it time to let go or yield to powers greater than ourselves?"

The failure to yield and accept "what is" is the psychological equivalent of a tight fist and clenched teeth. Most of us can recall the feeling of loosening the grip or relaxing the jaw. Again, we are faced with a paradox. When we "let go," we often develop greater capacity to do all that we are capable of to confront a situation. Most who have played sports know how performance is inhibited when we hold the bat, racquet or club too tightly. We lose the flow and grace that brings out our best.

Further, feeling that we are in control is spiritually deadening. When we hold onto the fantasy that we are in control, we are less likely to experience and feel deep gratitude for the gifts from the universe that come to us each day.

We are all only a blood test or a phone call away from heartbreaking or scary news that brings us face-to-face with something beyond our control. Yet, we have it within our reach to prepare for these eventualities. Each day provides an opportunity to gratefully contemplate our gifts and to develop our emotional and spiritual muscularity to determine when and how to persist and yield at the same time. In this regard, my wife's elegant and graceful journey through her diagnosis, treatment and death were inspirational to me.

As more challenging or discouraging experiences came her way, she would often say rhetorically, "What are you going to do?" This was not a flip or deflecting statement on her part. Rather, it was the result of years of meditation and spiritual reflection on life and loss and letting go.

Accepting the reality of what she was facing did nothing to diminish her wholehearted, good-humored and total commitment to available treatment options.

Many described her as waging a courageous battle. However, she never saw it as a battle and did not see herself as courageous. Rather, she surrendered to that which was larger than herself, did the best that she could, and never lost sight of the blessing that life had brought her.

May we all follow a path that provides such peace and release from suffering.

QUESTIONS: SURRENDER

Thoughts for contemplation, meditation or action:

1. How do you relate to the concept of "surrender" in your life? Positive? Negative? Why?

2. Are you facing anything in your life where surrendering or yielding might be a good idea?

3. What fears do you have about yielding or surrendering?

4. Do you know someone whom you admire for their ability to know when to persist and when to surrender to powers greater than themselves? What can you learn from them?

CHAPTER FOUR

PRAYER

What shall we pray for and to whom? There are those who are very comfortable asking for help in winning a ball game. Others pray for victory in war. On the other hand, some feel foolish using any prayer for intercession.

To whom shall we pray can get very complicated: God, Great Spirit, Divine Mother or Father, Eternal Consciousness? Our approach to prayer has to account for our relationship to the Higher Power as we understand it.

For me, it has come down to exploring my willingness to dialogue with a great unknowable force that has been here forever. Am I open to the possibility of an intimate, grateful and loving relationship with this unknown and eternal presence? Even if it can seem as though it's a one-way conversation?

There are those who say, if you only have one prayer, make it, "Thank You!" Frankly, if we were to lift our heads and say that many times throughout the day, the impact on our own and others' spirits would be significant. However, such ubiquitous expressions of gratitude can be scary when we know that we can't control when the next unwanted, unhappy experience will arrive at our doorstep.

I have chosen to take the risk and offer prayers of gratitude over and over again throughout each day. I have chosen to be grateful, even when I'm not in control. When I'm walking with a friend, I consider my comment, "What a beautiful day – we are so lucky," to be a prayer.

Years ago, I started a nightly prayer practice. Before going to sleep, I say, "May [*name*] be relieved of suffering. May they find peace. May they be well." Most nights I have 10 or 15 people whose life circumstances call for me to send them healing thoughts and energies. These prayers go out to near-in friends and family, as well as to more distant people that come to my attention through the news and other communications.

Skeptics may rightfully question where these prayers go and if they get answered. On the other hand, I can say without a doubt that the practice opens my heart and widens the circle of people for whom I feel loving compassion. On a more down-to-earth note, my heightened awareness of the suffering of others inspires me to make calls, drop by, and engage in other acts of kindness in the days following my prayers. These actions take me "out of my own skin" and make me appreciative of my good fortune.

Another function of prayer can be to quiet and slow us down. By taking the time to ask the "universe" to guide me – to help me know and lovingly respond to my calling; to help me see what the people in my life need from me – the chances increase that my eyes will be more open to the heartfelt needs of others.

In some cultures, prayer is the only inevitable duty: the daily recognition of the unseen, the eternal. There is a lot to be said for this ancient wisdom.

QUESTIONS: PRAYER

Thoughts for contemplation, meditation or action:

1. Would you like to know that you are in other people's prayers? Why? Why not?

2. Who are some people in your life that could use a prayer?

3. Is there someone in your life whom you admire who prays? Would you like to know more about how/why they pray?

4. Do you have a desire to expand the role of prayer in your life? What are you committed to trying?

CHAPTER FIVE

LOVE

Several religious and wisdom traditions speak of unconditional love. Nevertheless, many people lack the experience of love, having never really heard the words, "I love you" from important people who matter in their lives. Or, if one has heard the words, there may be a feeling that love is dependent on continuing to behave in a manner that earns the love.

It's no wonder that many of us spend much of our lives seeking to fill a hole in our hearts. Not trusting that love will come our way can set up a string of compensating behaviors. For instance, we may detach and not allow ourselves to get deeply connected so that we do not get hurt. Or, we give up so much of ourselves in search of love that we desperately desire, while still feeling cold and lonely.

Though these behaviors may not be exactly how your love story has unfolded, it is unlikely that your own path to finding love has not had ups and downs. Further, if one has been in the throes of a life challenge or loss, the absence of loving comfort and support may have been quite visible and painful.

About 15 years ago, I was conducting a workshop and discovered that a friend and colleague of mine had been with this group the previous month. When I mentioned my friend's name, the group members said, "Oh, we love him!" I was surprised at the impact that their expression of love for him had on me. I was convinced that they would not have said that about me, if the tables had been turned. It's entirely possible that they might have said, "Oh, we admire him. He's so smart!" I doubted that they would have said, "We love him!" This perception, accurate or not, was an awakening for me. It was clear that I had come to a time in my life when love was more important than admiration and respect. Further, it was clear that I had much more awareness of how to inspire admiration and respect than how to fulfill my desire for love.

Over the next few years of greater awareness, intention and focus on love, a revelation began to emerge. My journey needed to be reframed. Setting out on my true path meant switching from trying to find love to being loving, from trying to fill a hole in my heart to tenderly holding the hearts of others.

There is no guarantee that our love for others will be reciprocated. There is, however, a pretty good bet that not being fully loving will reduce the odds of love coming our way. More important, when we move from a utilitarian intention of giving love in order to receive love to a sacred intention to be loving, no matter the outcome, the game has changed. We will have come to the place of "being the unconditional love" that we yearn to experience. Paradoxically, this giving of our unconditional love starts a flow back that fills our own hearts.

There were many practices that I needed to engage to support and sustain my often-stumbling path towards love:

- I walked around for about two years with a beautiful, red crystal heart in my pocket. As I found myself drifting toward judgment of another, I reached in my pocket and imagined that I was "holding the other's heart."

- Before I sat down in front of a client for consulting or coaching support, I briefly meditated and pictured him or her in my mind utilizing "soft eyes and a loving heart."

- When I found myself feeling helpless or hopeless about a friend or family member's behavior toward me, I envisioned "unfreezing my heart," so that I could stay lovingly engaged.

- To keep my "love battery and reserves charged," I made certain that I intentionally noticed the sunrise each day, waiting to fill my heart with love; I didn't allow many days go by where I didn't listen to music, read a poem or see a piece of art that brought a tear to my eye; and I took every moment possible to look in to the eyes of friends and family members who were full of love and walking ahead of me on this path.

Love is often called the first rule of a spiritual life. A practice of love requires full-hearted commitment and attention. Love is the reward itself. When faced with pain and loss, love lets us understand that even a dismal picture carries possibility.

QUESTIONS: LOVE

Thoughts for contemplation, meditation or action:

1. Who are the greatest sources of love in your life? Do they know how important their love is to you?

2. What are the ways in which you demonstrate your love? Are there things that you would like to add to your repertoire of loving behaviors?

3. What gets in the way of your being your most loving self?

4. What activities in your life fill your heart with love? Do you do these things enough?

CHAPTER SIX

BEING PRESENT

There are those moments when it seems as though we would rather be anywhere than where we are. Common spoken or unspoken feelings are:

- "If I can just get through this day."

- "I have such a bad month of travel coming up."

- "When will this ordeal be over?"

- "I've got so much to do, when can I get out of here?"

- "I don't have time to listen to this; I've got to get going!"

Those are future-focused wanderings, but the past also invades the present:

- "I wish we could do this the way we did before."

- "Yesterday was so beautiful. Where did the sunshine go?"

- "We had so much fun together, once."

- "They don't make them like they used to."

There is certainly a place for dreams of the future and fond remembrances of the past. Our challenge is to not allow the past or the future to unduly distract us from the present moment. There are those who assert that there is no past and there is no future. There is only the present.

Mindfulness meditation helps us notice when we are present and when we are elsewhere; whether we are peaceful or scattered; and patterns revealed in the comings and goings of our wandering minds. In meditation, there is no intention to stop or control these diversions. Rather, the benefit lies in simple awareness. And heightened awareness carries the potential for choice and change. What kind of change? Awareness of our patterns opens the door to greater capacity to stay present. Further, it becomes clearer whether where and with whom we find ourselves is nourishing and satisfying.

As we age, we have less interest in missing the cherished moments in our lives. We no longer want to rush through the days. We yearn to slow them down. We want to be fully present for every one of our waning hours. As we have less time, we do not want to miss anything by distracting ourselves with what's coming next or recollections of earlier times.

Let's not take many showers without noticing how really good they feel. Let's savor our meals. Let's enjoy the beauty in the landscapes that we drive through as we run errands. All activities can be mindfulness meditations supporting our capacity to be fully present each moment.

As my wife's treatment for leukemia proceeded, I didn't know if she would survive. However, I was very certain that I did not want to miss one moment of whatever time we had left. Each day became a mindfulness meditation, where I became intensely aware of mental distractions that catapulted me to the future or jerked me back to the past. Many times each day I reminded myself, "Right here, right now."

I sometimes feel sad that it required the threat of my wife's death to inspire me to such a commitment to "all in:" i.e., a right-here, right-now, loving presence. But I take heart in the fact that I had laid the groundwork to allow me to bring myself fully to her, when I was called to do so.

With intent, attention and daily practice, each of us has the opportunity to gently and lovingly bring ourselves into full contact with each present moment. And we will be ready to deeply experience, with our loved ones, the joys and losses that life brings our way.

QUESTIONS: BEING PRESENT

Thoughts for contemplation, meditation or action:

1. Are you aware of your wandering patterns? Do you tend to drift more to the future or the past? Why do you think that is true?

2. Do you have a sense of a "ticking clock?" Does that affect your desire to be more present each moment?

3. Are there people in your life who would like you to be more present when you are with them?

4. Where are you likely to not be fully present? Home? Work? Social gatherings? Other? Why? Do you want to do something about this awareness?

CHAPTER SEVEN

BELIEF

Many great teachers and prophets have walked this earth. I suspect that a fair number would be surprised and saddened to see what has become of their teachings. During their time with us, most were intending to offer comfort in a world of mystery and uncertainty; a vision for finding higher purpose; guidance as we struggle with decisions of right and wrong; a pathway to love and respect for self and others; and a deep sense of awe and gratitude for the gift of life.

As a young person learning about many of the practices, rituals and rules that believers had created, I was, at times, incredulous. I couldn't imagine that a God would care about who did or did not eat pork; whether or not I had fish on Friday; or how many Hail Mary's were recited. I was particularly put off by the claims that only certain believers were bound for heaven while others were damned.

Many share my skepticism about some of the rules that structure their religion's doctrine. Some choose to stay members of their groups, simply ignoring the things that they don't believe or care about. Others cannot tolerate the dissonance and find it necessary to dissociate, often with a sense of great loss for abandoning what had been nourishing about their religious community.

A friend asked me if I believed in mediums – those who serve as intermediaries between the living and the dead. I told her that for the past decade I had opened myself to exploring the limits of non-rational experience (e.g., psychics, palm readers, visiting sacred places, etc.), but that I hadn't gotten to mediums. She went on to explain to me that she had decided to "experiment with believing" and see how it affected her. Does it help her gain insight into herself or others? Does it expand loving compassion for herself and others?

Was she humbled in the face of the great mystery? Does it have an impact on her sense of thankfulness and gratitude?

I was deeply touched by her idea of "experimenting with believing," while staying solidly grounded in criteria for reflection on living within that belief.

In this spirit, I find myself joining my Jewish friends for Friday night Shabbat and reveling weekly in the wonders of creation. Easter worship services serve to ignite my passion for renewal and rebirth. Sitting with others in celebration of a solstice creates a sense of reverence for the passing of one season and the beginning of another. I join my Unitarian friends to take a stand against social injustices.

What do I believe? First and foremost, I believe that spending time in communities of sacred, shared good intent is essential. Moreover, I believe that rituals to celebrate life events, acknowledge our gifts, and soothe us during times of loss are good for the soul. I feel no risk for damnation. If there is a God, I am confident that this is what He or She would want us to do.

As children, we are wise enough to talk to birds, animals and trees. We feel a deep connection to everything. We take joy in all of these conversations.

As a very young child, my wife wrote, "I love God," on the brick in the front of her family home. Her passionate proclamation remains there to this day. No matter how far my wife wandered from the dogma of her faith, she never lost that childlike connection with creation.

We all have the opportunity to engage in sacred practices that open our hearts and guide our actions, even in the face of our doubts.

QUESTIONS: BELIEF

Thoughts for contemplation, meditation or action:

1. What do you believe?

2. How are the religious experiences of your youth influencing your current beliefs?

3. Do your beliefs provide you support during times of loss and grief? Do they allow you to support others?

4. Do your beliefs make you a more loving and compassionate person?

CHAPTER EIGHT

KARMA

"What goes around comes around" is an oft-stated warning. It is usually a caution that our misbehavior will come back to haunt us in the future. Sometimes, however, it is an encouragement that our good deeds will not go unrewarded.

In Hinduism and Buddhism, the belief is that the sum of a person's actions in this and previous states of existence determines his or her fate in future existences. This leads to an endless cycle of rebirth, with the potential for enlightenment.

Though past or future existences are just speculation, I have little doubt that our accumulated thoughts and actions have significant effect on what comes back our way. Further, we have many opportunities to be "reborn" in this lifetime, as we move toward creating our "best selves."

Practices that heighten our awareness of our intentions, behavior and impact on others go a long way toward shaping the karmic field in which we find ourselves. Likewise, a community of people seeking to become their best selves creates a relational field that may not be nirvana, but is the next best thing – a wise and compassionate form of heaven on earth. The blessings of this kind of community that holds and supports one another during life's challenges is immeasurable.

Creation of this "karmic reality" begins with a deep commitment to a fearless examination of our own thoughts, actions and behaviors. It includes joining communities of people who openly share our hopes, dreams and vulnerabilities. When our behaviors hurt others, we are called on to abandon a false sense of innocence and to make amends.

We are stretched and tested when facing betrayal or the need to forgive.

At the age of 74, I am certain that God hasn't finished me. I am not yet the friend I want to be. I am not yet the father, consultant or coach that I want to be. This is not a problem to be solved. If I were to die tomorrow, I would not feel unfinished or shameful about my progress in this life. Nevertheless, since I have some more time, I look forward to several more "rebirths" on the way to being my best self. I cherish the possibility of ever-expanding capacity for loving responses to all of my life partners.

In addition, I take great comfort in the fact that I am surrounded by likeminded fellow travelers and, together, we are co-creating a future that will lovingly hold us, as our destiny unfolds before us.

With a commitment to love, sacred self-examination and a deep belief in the potential for creating loving communities, we are all better supported for whatever the future may hold.

QUESTIONS: KARMA

Thoughts for contemplation, meditation or action:

1. Is awareness of your impact on others a strength of yours? How might you get more input on that question? Do you want to get more input?

2. How do you think your own thoughts, actions and behaviors are influencing what is coming back to you?

3. How would you like to influence the "karmic field" that comes back to you? With whom? How?

4. Are you part of any communities that are intentionally trying to build a nourishing relational field? If not, would you like to start such a community?

CHAPTER NINE

DESIRE

Exploring our relationship to powerful human desires provides a significant opportunity for personal growth and spiritual transformation.

The motivational aspect of desire is an undeniable part of all human actions. Desire can propel us toward goals, advancement and abundant living. On the other hand, our cravings can be the source of great suffering.

Desires on which our happiness appears to hinge can lead to fear, loneliness, greed and emptiness. Desires that set us free include the quest for goodness, wisdom and connection to life's great mysteries.

We can engage in practices that refocus our desires and create space between these desires and our actions – space that allows us to consider the underlying source of the desire. Awareness, reason and higher purpose can interact and help us determine if our desires are fueled by emptiness or by love.

Each day, we experience many moments where we are confronted with wishes, longing and deep desires – strong feelings to possess something or make something happen. The intensity of our feelings can rise to the level of craving, coveting and jealousy. These feelings are fueled by the ever-increasing sophistication and bombardment of marketing and advertising.

Early in my working life, when I had little money to spend on non-essentials, I could justify my yearnings as the natural desire to progress and keep up with the Joneses. However, as my career flourished and I no longer had to forgo many wants, it became clearer that satisfying these desires was no longer a simple matter of having more money. There would never be enough money. This feeling of deficit could not be solved by accumulating more possessions. My increasing income level did not liberate me from the grip of these yearnings. There were many people with less money than I who seemed to be happier with their lot in life. Achieving a peaceful relationship with these desires was not going to be determined by my economic status. I may have been deflecting some anxieties with housing, clothes, entertainment, gifts and travel, but the relief was always temporary.

Sobered by my realization that I could not buy my way out of these feelings, I decided it was time to slow down, take stock and heighten my awareness of whether I was motivated by my emptiness or the fullness and gratefulness of my good fortune. With some reflection, deep breathing and distance, it became possible to undertake a more enduring examination and focus my attention on underlying causes for any loneliness or emptiness.

As the years move on, we face accumulating losses. Our desire to hold on, change what happens, accomplish a goal or acquire something before dying may intensify. However, informed by years of reflecting on what we have and really need, we learn that we are more than what we seek. We are more than our desires. We discover that the goodness in and around us becomes satisfying, becomes enough.

QUESTIONS: DESIRE

Thoughts for contemplation, meditation or action:

1. How has your own or others' desire, craving, coveting or jealousy affected your life?

2. What kinds of things do you do to slow down and step back, when desire may be influencing decisions or behaviors that are not good for you or others?

3. What current desire are you "under the spell of" that might be a problem?

4. What practices have you engaged in that help you make peace with whatever you have/ can't have in life?

CHAPTER TEN

STILLNESS

Calm, cool and collected seems like such a desirable state of mind. However, it's a condition that is easier wished for than achieved.

Many of our lives involve constant busyness, back-to-back appointments, intense contact and limited time between engagements. For some, this lifestyle is very satisfying and quite productive. For these people, a less-full schedule might feel like a prelude to boredom or wasted time. Others yearn for more quiet and uncommitted moments, but do not make it happen.

In the end, the true measure of stillness is independent of whether our lives are packed full or more sedate. We seek the kind of stillness that allows us to have full access to our true selves; that brings our undivided attention to our feelings, motives, fears and other enduring life themes; that allows us to "empty" and be more receptive to everything in and around us.

Though it is possible to be quiet and centered inside, when we are in a high action mode, it is unlikely that we can develop this physical and emotional capability without stepping back to make time for physical and mental retreat and reflection. What we learn during these reflective breaks can be carried forward into the busier times in our lives.

With activities such as yoga, meditation, listening to music, kayaking or walks, we have the chance to develop and appreciate the gifts available in these quiet moments that we create. In day-to-day activities, with intention, attention and focus, we can cook, paint, repair cars or do housework, even as we achieve relief from "monkey mind" and fantasy excursions to the past or future. We can be fully present, calm, cool and collected, but it takes practice.

As time goes on, this quiet internal space becomes a high-energy place – not the prison of boredom that some may have feared. This quiet, empty place is full of electric contact with ourselves, others and the entire environment of which we are part.

From this still and centered place, we can choose to jump into the fray or sit back and observe. Whatever our choice, we invoke in ourselves and others a sense of calm, confidence, connection and authentic presence. We do not lose ourselves and we do not rush past others. We are fully present.

As the years roll on, life circumstances are likely to usher more quiet, less active spaces into our lives; people die or move away; life partners are lost; careers end; physical capabilities become limited. If we have made way for stillness earlier in our lives, these losses and changes will be less daunting. Not only can we find peace with these changes, we can learn to cherish this quieter time in our lives.

QUESTIONS: STILLNESS

Thoughts for contemplation, meditation or action:

1. What role does stillness play in your physical and emotional well-being?

2. Do you feel as though you have enough stillness time in your life?

3. What interrupts or interferes with the stillness in your life that you wish to have?

4. What are you inspired to do to create or sustain the amount of stillness that you require?

CHAPTER ELEVEN

EMBODIMENT

Our bodies are constantly sending messages, and we can become practiced at listening. We can learn that a trauma or loss has a bigger impact on us than our mind is telling us. There are signals that the social or physical environment in which we are living or working is toxic or unsafe. We can sense that we are "making ourselves small" because of the echoes of a disturbing event from our past.

Some of us have strong body awareness when we are alone, but we lose touch with ourselves when we become socially engaged. This disconnect robs us of valuable signals that can be used to enhance our relational success, and protect us from taking action or making decisions that are not in our best interest. As we dance with others and the world around us, our ability to stay connected to our bodies has a significant impact on our health, well-being and success.

Though we all understand that the separation between body and mind is imaginary, we can still be aware when our minds seem to be hijacking our bodies as we are about to do or say something that just doesn't feel right. Perhaps we notice a jump in our heart rate; we complain of a stiff neck or a burning gut; or we hear our voice tremble. These physical messages can be very helpful if we are attuned to our bodies. On the other hand, we may recognize these feelings but ignore them because we do not see them as important.

Most of us spend a lot of time in our heads. It takes discipline to keep calling ourselves back to our bodies. Regularly attending to our breathing; keeping our feet firmly on the ground; and aligning the spine and pelvis are practices that bring us back home to our physical selves and ready us to meet life's challenges.

The importance of this physiological awareness extends well beyond our own self-care. We are all actors in a play, where people make meaning out of our every movement. They react to our posture and all aspects of our physical presentation. We send messages through our embodied self. Sometimes these messages are exactly what we intended. On other occasions, we may be blind to the impact that our physical presence evokes. Our presence can be intimidating. We may present ourselves in ways that diminish our influence. Our impact may be off-putting or inviting. If we want to fully realize the potential in all relationships, it behooves us to truly see what others are noticing. We can do this by staying alert to verbal and nonverbal cues; asking for feedback; and participating in body awareness workshops or other experiences that help us get direct, open and honest reactions to our presence.

In the end, our body awareness allows us to feel fully alive and deeply connected to ourselves and the world that surrounds us. Since life is short and everything and everybody comes and goes, we want to take in every delicious moment and make intimate contact with ourselves, others and everything we touch. We can achieve this "touching" contact with full sensory access to the glorious body that we have been given.

QUESTIONS: EMBODIMENT

Thoughts for contemplation, meditation or action:

1. What interests you about the concept of embodiment? Why?

2. What practices do you have to heighten your body awareness?

3. What warning signals does your body send if you are stressed, in an undesirable situation, losing your confidence, etc.? Do you regularly heed these messages?

4. What do you know about your physical presence that may be getting in your way? What might you do about that?

CHAPTER TWELVE

RELATIONSHIP INVESTING

It's probably wise to have a balanced portfolio of relationships. A healthy portfolio includes people with whom we share long histories and fond memories and those who make us laugh. Others in our personal portfolio may have the same taste in entertainment, and there are those to whom we turn for advice and counsel. Some people can fulfill many of our needs, but there are few who can be counted upon to be all-purpose.

Regardless of the mix or breadth of our portfolio, we always want to include those with whom we can share our most intimate thoughts, dreams, fears and vulnerabilities. It is this kind of friendship that can at times befuddle or discourage us. Many feel that these kinds of people are few and far between. We may be reeling from the disappointment of one more shallow conversation about topics that have little poignancy or apparent potential for intimacy. On the other hand, we may be reveling in a uniquely satisfying connection, only to feel sadness about how rare these engagements have been for us.

Set against the backdrop of such disappointing experiences, it can be difficult to imagine that there are many people out there who are ready, willing and able to build deep and enduring relationships. When I have participated in groups that have just had a deep and intimate experience together, it is very common to hear someone say, "This has been wonderful and so rare. I wish there were more people who wanted to connect this way!"

For some, then, it is very daunting to invest heavily in relationships, with the specter of failure and feelings of scarcity haunting us. Yet, we must take the risk. We do not want to find ourselves dealing with the losses and challenges that life brings unsupported by loving and kind people in our lives. We don't have to satisfy with one or two; the more, the better.

What does a good relationship investment strategy look like? A very experienced financial investor once told me that if you hit one out of five times on high-risk/high-payoff investments, you are doing very well. So, we start with the mindset that we should expect some failures, but the payoff is worth it. Next, we need to screen our investments to give us a better chance to win big. In looking for relationships to invest in, watch for people who:

- Have shown themselves to be listeners;

- Offer small bits of intimate information;

- May be quicker than average to hug;

- Share an awareness of an area for their personal development;

- Express gratitude or appreciation for something you have done; or

- Offer assistance or a kind hand without being asked.

Any of these characteristics is a signal that investment on your part may pay high dividends.

As you select people in whom you wish to invest, you should consider the following investment best practices:

- Think about engaging in the practices that attracted you to them.

- Regularly inquire as to what is going on in their lives; track what they share with you; and surprise them by checking back to see how things turned out.

- Don't keep a scorecard of whose turn it is to call or make contact. When you are missing them or want to connect, reach out.

- Don't withhold sharing difficult things that are going on in your life because you know that they have their own troubles.

- Never pass up the chance to tell them how much they mean to you.

It's impossible to overstate the significance of these deep relationships during life's challenging times. It's well worth the investment, the failures and the reinvestment.

With courage, risk-taking and lifelong investment, we all can be comforted in the loving arms of a community of supporters when times are difficult. Equally important, we get to feel the deep love and connection that can only come by being on the other end when we open our hearts and arms to those who need our understanding, care and support.

QUESTIONS: RELATIONSHIP INVESTING

Thoughts for contemplation, meditation or action:

1. Do you have a feeling of abundance or (scarcity) as it relates to the availability of people with whom you can have deep and intimate relationships? Why?

    yes

2. What do you do or not do that contributes to your success in building close relationships?

3. What do you do or not do that may interfere with building and sustaining close relationships?

    self deprecate

4. At this time, in what relationships do you want to invest more? Less?

    Jordan + Ethan

CHAPTER THIRTEEN

EXPRESSING FEELINGS

Some of us grew up in families with parents or other family members who were completely unable to deal with feelings. Further, there were strong messages, spoken or unspoken, that we were to keep our feelings to ourselves. Others had a parent or family member who was unable to regulate his or her feelings, leaving them exposed to intense, inappropriate and constant emotional outbursts.

It's no wonder that many of us are left with great confusion about if, when, how and to whom we should express our pain, vulnerability, sadness or even love.

We can struggle with any number of worries. We may:

- Not want to come off as a helpless victim;

- Be certain that we will not be listened to or misunderstood;

- Want to avoid being seen as someone who wallows in his/her sorrows;

- Fear that we will meet unsympathetic ears and be harshly judged;

- Fret that we will be burdening others with our troubles;

- Not wish to ask for help and then have our request be unmet; or

- Be afraid that if we open our floodgate, we will go down an emotional rat hole.

To further complicate matters, if we stuff our feelings, over time we can find ourselves unable to access these feelings. We can tell people what we "think," but what we truly feel is hidden from us and others in our lives.

There is abundant research that supports the importance of expressing our feelings in support of emotional and physical well-being. Conversely, the role that bottled up emotions plays in setting us on the road to depression, loneliness and rage, is well documented.

Most of us know in our hearts that we need to talk to each other.

We need to share our pains and disappointments. We need to be available to listen openly and tenderly to others. We need to be available to each other even when there is nothing they or we can do but listen and "be there." Expressing ourselves allows us to feel our pain but not become it.

Building the emotional capacity for expressing our feelings requires observation, experiments and practice. We must learn from people who have more access to their feelings. We can notice how, when and to whom they open themselves. We can be on high alert for those who appear to be sincerely asking how we are doing and experiment with giving them more authentic responses to their inquiry. Moreover, we must pay attention to how good it feels to be listened to and understood – perhaps inspiring us to expand the depth and reach of our experiments.

Life does not get easier, as time marches onward. Most of us know friends and loved ones who are facing life challenges that cry out for companionship, a kind ear and a caring heart. With intention, courage and lifelong experiments, we become able to express, honor and release our own feelings and be that invaluable resource to others.

QUESTIONS: EXPRESSING FEELINGS

Thoughts for contemplation, meditation or action:

1. What did you learn early in life that stands in the way of expressing your feelings? *was often tactless as a child + young adult — overcompensated*

2. What joy or sorrow is most in your heart at this time that you would like to share with others?

3. Who are your best candidates with whom you can share your true feelings? Do they know how much you value them for that gift? *SW Martha L*

4. Who needs you at this at time to be available to listen to their feelings?

CHAPTER FOURTEEN

CHANGE

Recently, I found a ten-year-old picture of my wife, Karen, our two beloved cats, and me. They are all gone – so is JFK, Martin Luther King, Elvis, Maya Angelou, Bob Hoskins, Philip Seymour Hoffman and Casey Kasem. During a 2013 visit to my hometown, I discovered that my old family home had been razed. When I listen to music award programs, many of the songs and winners are unrecognizable. I can't name all of the countries that made up the former Soviet Union. It's difficult not to see the turmoil in the Middle East as a possible prelude to disastrous change.

My world as I knew it no longer exists.

As we age and the personal, political and cultural world around us changes, it can be difficult to avoid becoming dour and pessimistic. The feeling that "the world is going to hell in a hand basket" may, occasionally, creep into our minds and conversations.

The practices that we use to engage with our changing worlds can have an enormous impact on our states of mind and our ability to join in the change. Some of these practices include:

- **Acceptance.** Several years ago, a friend referred to himself and me as dinosaurs. At first, I was taken aback and resisted the label. On reflection, his statement rang true. He was suggesting that we simply accept the idea that the education, life experience and emotional development of our kids and grandkids make them better suited to live and flourish in this changed world. We certainly have wisdom and contributions to add and pass on before checking out. However, a peaceable relationship with the fact that we are leaving; they are inheriting the world we have left behind; and the world is in their good hands, frees us to add our remaining value while deeply appreciating and affirming their readiness to carry on.

- **Flexibility.** Keeping ourselves "loose in the saddle" about our beliefs and world views may be even more challenging than stretching our aging muscles. It has been said that the highest form of human development is recognizing the incompleteness of our most strongly held views. It's not that our views are wrong. It's just that they are incomplete. There is something about the views of others that would be wise for us to consider – something about which they are worried or fearful that deserves our attention. Supported by this stance, we do not demonize those with whom we differ. We develop more nuanced ability to see the value others add; thus changes sponsored by others feel less threatening.

- **Curiosity.** My wife, Karen, was a pathfinder for me in this area. She had endless curiosity about the world around her. She wanted to know everything she could about how young people were using technology and what music they were enjoying. New TV programs served as her window into emerging cultural patterns. Business, science and celebrity magazines all captured her attention. Her conversations were laced with, "Tell me more. How does that work? What do you like about that? Where do you think that is taking us?" Her inquiry was pure and without judgment. The potential that existed in all things sparked her excitement and left little room for fear of change.

- **Creativity.** As things that we have cherished disappear, we can be soothed and invigorated by what we create. Our music-making, painting, writing, pottery and gardens connect us to a generative part in ourselves. Our support for organizations and people who are addressing our issues of concern arouses our productive juices. These creative endeavors may arise from our grief or loss. For instance, we may join in the fight against a disease that has taken a loved one or use our creativity to express feelings that we and others may be having difficulty accessing. As time passes, the creativity born of painful changes can become a practice that awakens us to the beauty and goodness that still exist in the world.

Acceptance, flexibility, curiosity and creativity offer a pathway to living more peacefully and generatively amidst an accumulation of changes. Nevertheless, to support our journey through life's changes, we still must rely upon core, underlying practices that keep us connected to our awe and gratitude for the gift of life and our loving compassion for those that still grace our lives to further support our journey through life's changes.

QUESTIONS: CHANGE

Thoughts for contemplation, meditation or action:

1. What characteristics or behaviors have supported you through past changes?

2. What is changing right now that you are having the most trouble accepting?

3. What do you know you need to do to prepare yourself to live with the changes that are coming your way?

4. To whom do you turn for support in the face of difficult changes? Do they know how much it means to you that they are there for you?

CHAPTER FIFTEEN

RITUALS

A friend says goodbye to a 30-year job and slips quietly off to his retirement, suggesting that he doesn't want anyone to make a fuss. Two gay lovers whose families do not support their marriage can't bring themselves to have a wedding, so they settle for going by themselves to a justice of the peace. Two poor, working parents who cannot afford to take time off from their jobs have to miss their son's high school graduation. Very, very sad!

A 16-year-old boy beams with delight as his parents, grandparents and friends come to celebrate the completion of his yearlong rite-of-passage experience. Fourteen people pray, sing, tell sweet stories and whisper loving goodbyes, as they sit in vigil for an unconscious dying woman. Friends about to build a new home on land that has not been occupied since the Native Americans lived there, hold a ceremony to ask the ancestors for their blessing and permission to proceed. Very, very touching!

Opportunities to make major and everyday moments sacred present themselves all the time. These ubiquitous occasions transcend cultures and time. They celebrate beginnings, endings and passages. With words, objects, music and art they make a moment or place special. Through behaviors, symbols and acts that are performed before, during or after a meaningful event, they build community and create customs and traditions.

Through rituals we have the chance to fully experience the holy meaning of the current moment. And we can make a timeless connection to all that came before. Our joy can be shared and deepened during moments of celebration and our grief and anxiety relieved by new and ancient traditions.

For some to embrace the beauty to be found in rituals, they may have to recover from repetitive, mind-numbing demands of their earlier religious training. Others may feel reluctant to engage in "touchy-feely" activities that seem at odds with their commitment to rationality.

There is the old saying that sometimes we have to "fake it 'til we make it." It may require us to risk surrendering ourselves to experiences that magically allow our spirits to be stirred and our hearts lifted and carried away.

We can all grow in our ability to be receptive individuals who seek to unblock the dams in us that inhibit the free flow of our emotions that rituals can evoke. These emotions allow us to celebrate and affirm the accomplishments and events in the lives of those we love. They also create a loving community space to hold ourselves and others who are suffering a loss.

QUESTIONS: RITUALS

Thoughts for contemplation, meditation or action:

1. What has been your past response to rituals? Drawn toward? Resistant? Why?

2. What's the most significant experience that you have ever had with a ritual? Positive? Negative?

3. What's going on in your life that might warrant a ritual?

4. What's going on in a friend's or family member's life that might be celebrated or acknowledged with a ritual?

CHAPTER SIXTEEN

NO-SELF

The Buddha teaches that a person is merely a collection of earth, water, fire and air that comes together; is thought of as a person; and then breaks up and decays.

I sort of understand but I don't fully get it. I have such a strong sense of what is me and what is mine.

I can look at rainbows and see how all the elements come together to create such a beautiful "reality" and quickly fade into the whole. Watching waves rise and fall provides additional evidence of things aggregating, appearing and disappearing.

Embracing the concept of "no-self" offers the promise of reduced suffering. Reportedly, if we understand that the self is only a convention, then problems are finished. There are no problems. There is no self to solve the non-problems. No suffering. No one to die – only the inevitable collapse of earth, water, air and fire.

When I reflect on the idea of no-self, I see the "truth" of these teachings and I can feel the release that can come from embracing this no-self, no-me, no-mine philosophy. Nevertheless, my ego quickly kicks in to reinforce my powerful self-identity. I resist the thought that I and all that I accomplish and acquire in the world will decay and disappear.

When I was a kid, I used to think of people being formed by some great spirit dipping a cup in to a universal ocean of human spirit and then pouring us back into the ocean, at the time of death. Perhaps because my younger self had not developed many trappings and attachments, I was less threatened by this appearing and disappearing.

I want to understand this, but it is so hard. It is something that I expect to reflect upon for the rest of my life. It is clearly my spiritual cutting edge. However, my contemplation of this "no-self" does give me some glimpse of what it feels like to relax my grip. If there is no me and mine, then losses have less sting. Whatever we may attain or accomplish is subject to decay and loss, so don't get too worked up about it.

I don't know how far I will get in achieving this wisdom and tranquility, as well as the peace that comes with full acceptance that I and everything else rises and ultimately ceases. However, I'm convinced that, as we reflect on these issues, there is great potential for loosening the grip on our egos; preparing us for all that comes and goes; and reducing the suffering about our own passing.

Reflecting and meditating on these issues opens our hearts to the great mystery of being human and connects us to all those before us who have yearned for understanding and the reduction of suffering.

QUESTIONS: NO-SELF

Thoughts for contemplation, meditation or action:

1. Do you find the concept of "no-self" scary? Comforting? Other?

2. How are you impacted by the fact that everything you accomplish and attain in life is subject to decay and loss?

3. How does a strong attachment to "me or mine" show up in your life?

4. How might loosening your grip on your ego or possessions benefit you at this time in your life?

CHAPTER SEVENTEEN

COMPASSION

A friend once invited me to read the newspaper for an entire week, with this stipulation: I had to keep my heart wide open. I tried, but at the time I was unable to do it. There is so much suffering, so much pain. It felt like I just had to turn away.

Watching family members and friends who are enduring heartache can be unbearable. For a long time, I thought that the only way I could be with them was to "freeze my heart."

One definition of compassion is the emotion we feel in response to the pain of others that motivates a desire to help. Is it any wonder that we can become immobilized or emotionally numbed when we face suffering about which there is little we can do or fix?

The etymology of "compassion" is from the Latin word "compassio" meaning "co-suffering." This suggests to me that we must develop a compassionate relationship to our own suffering before we can affirm our solidarity with another's pain. However, I have heard many people say something like, "I don't want anyone to feel sorry for me." I have come to believe that such a remark can be an indication that these individuals don't know how to experience or express their own suffering. They don't want to be trapped into feeling sorry for themselves. Likewise, they don't want anyone to think they are feeling sorry for themselves. Sadly, denying their own pain can result in an inability to be compassionate to themselves, as well as serving to fend off any compassion that might be flowing their way.

A friend in my men's group very emotionally reported that he really wanted to be able to be more compassionate. Again, is it any wonder that so many of us struggle to unleash this powerful yearning to connect deeply with the pain of those we love, let alone the trauma around the planet? In order to do so, we seek to make peace with what we can't do anything about; we find ways to protect ourselves from being overwhelmed, as we unfreeze our hearts; and we open ourselves to receiving the compassion that comes our way, confident that we will not fall into a pit of self-pity.

Bill Clinton was sometimes ridiculed for saying, "I feel your pain." I have no idea how true that statement was for him. However, I applaud the intention. On this path toward compassion, we make our way in the direction of deep comradeship and human contact. Our loving kindness toward ourselves and others flourishes. We become receivers of what we send out.

QUESTIONS: COMPASSION

Thoughts for contemplation, meditation or action:

1. Do you consider yourself a compassionate person? Why? Why not?

2. Do you think that you are compassionate towards yourself? Why? Why not?

3. How are you affected by the suffering of others? How does that support your ability to "be there" for them?

4. What do you think will be required for you to expand your capacity for compassion for yourself and other?

CONCLUSION: IT'S NEVER TOO LATE

In my introduction, I pointed to the accumulating losses that occur as we reach middle age and beyond, the kinds of changes that can derail us emotionally and physically. I asked the provocative question, "What are we counting on to develop a more peaceable relationship to these losses?" I spoke of feeling "called" to write this book. That calling is rooted in the deep gratitude that I feel for the enduring sense of love and well-being that has accompanied me throughout the illness and loss of my dear wife, Karen, and other challenging life circumstances in recent years. I wanted to share my discoveries and awarenesses. I hoped to pass on whatever part of my experience was transferable.

I recognize that some of my experience is a pure gift of temperament that came with no effort of my own. I was granted a certain resiliency as my birthright. Further, I have been blessed to have many teachers, mentors and friends who have modeled and taught me enduring lessons: lessons that deepened my self-awareness and self-acceptance. These learnings enhanced my ability to develop deep and loving relationships and provided guidance that has led me to a spiritual path.

Though we each are born with different dispositions and follow a variety of paths chosen and accidental, I have come to believe that there is a something that may benefit all of us, a practice that can reduce our suffering and expand our capacity for loving kindness. This overarching practice is "mindfulness." And it is never too late to pursue this exercise that offers such possibility to bring us joy and reduce our suffering.

Mindfulness can be described as anything that we do to support intentional, accepting and nonjudgmental attention to our emotions, thoughts and sensations in the present moment. It also includes practices that heighten our loving connection to all that is larger than ourselves. For many, mindfulness meditation evokes images of sitting, eyes closed, cross-legged on a cushion. If the truth be told, I have not been very successful with long-term sitting meditations. I have not given up, because the payoff is undeniable. And I recommend it for all. If you haven't started, begin now.

However, I take heart in the discovery that mindfulness can be accessible outside a formal setting. The practices, skills and techniques used in meditation can be brought into every moment of our lives: showering, cooking, running, working, gardening, eating, housework, etc. With intention, we can use these daily activities to reflect and explore our awareness of how the themes in this book may relate to our lives and struggles.

I invite you to consider which of the topics in this book feel most compelling to you. Do they appeal to you because you are well on the way in this area and want to maximize the payoff? Because it feels like an area that has escaped your attention? Because you see the potential for reducing your suffering? Because you yearn for the potential for love that may be possible?

As we go about each day, we can take every opportunity to intentionally and non-judgmentally focus our attention on the emotions, thoughts and sensations that we are experiencing related to these complex and intertwined life issues.

Then we do it over and over again. This sacred process opens our hearts to the peace and possibilities that exist in each moment of our lives. It's never too late!

EPILOGUE

As my mindfulness journey unfolded over the years, I found myself creating a mantra to guide my daily reflections. The stanzas, as they appear below, were added in the order that they appear and reflect my emerging consciousness over time. There were often years between the creation of the stanzas, as I took time to fully embrace and live into the previous reflection.

"I am full of awe, gratitude and loving kindness.
I am well. I am confident, peaceful and at ease...Thank you!
Eternal Spirit, into thy loving hands I surrender my soul and destiny.
May I know and lovingly respond to my calling, today."

I find myself saying all or part of this reflection a number of times each day. It supports my attention to the sacred journey. Moreover, I am very curious and excited to discover what new stanza will emerge to guide the days ahead.

I offer my mantra as a tiny glimpse into my personal spiritual path; as an invitation to craft your own guiding reflections to support your journey; and as a gift, in the event that what I have created may resonate and support your heart and soul.

ABOUT THE AUTHOR

Richard W. Hallstein is Managing Director of Consulting Partners, a consulting and training consortium headquartered in Yarmouth, Maine. Previously, he was CEO of McLagan International, after spending many years in banking and retailing as a senior executive in line management, human resources and strategic planning. His formal training is in education, organization development and Gestalt therapy.

Hallstein's previous publications include *Memoirs of a Recovering Autocrat* – a self-revealing and intimate story of the author's journey to overcome autocratic and controlling leadership behaviors on the way toward a new vision for participative management, in which everyone can profit from collaboration and shared responsibility.

In this new book, he continues his tradition of intimate and self-revealing stories by sharing confessions, personal experiences and hopeful possibilities for dealing with the painful and accumulating losses that are part of each of our lives.

Hallstein continues his consulting and coaching work in Maine, deeply informed by the leadership lessons from his earlier book and the spiritual revelations shared in his newest offering: *Life, Love and Loss: Pathways to Peace and Possibilities*.